United States Government Accountability Office

Report to Congressional Committees

I0411569

September 2014

AIR TRAFFIC CONTROL SYSTEM

Selected Stakeholders' Perspectives on Operations, Modernization, and Structure

GAO-14-770

AIR TRAFFIC CONTROL SYSTEM

Selected Stakeholders' Perspectives on Operations, Modernization, and Structure

Highlights of GAO-14-770, a report to congressional committees

Why GAO Did This Study

Over the past two decades, U.S. aviation stakeholders have debated whether FAA should be the entity in the United States that operates and modernizes the ATC system. During this period, GAO reported on challenges FAA has faced in operating and modernizing the ATC system. FAA reorganized several times in attempts to improve its performance and implement an initiative to modernize the ATC system, known as NextGen. Recent budgetary pressures have rekindled industry debate about FAA's efficiency in operating and modernizing the ATC system.

GAO was asked to gather U.S. aviation industry stakeholder views on the operation and modernization of the current ATC system. This report provides perspectives from a wide range of stakeholders on

(1) the performance of the ATC system and the NextGen modernization initiative and any challenges FAA may face in managing these activities and

(2) potential changes that could improve the performance of the ATC system, including the NextGen modernization initiative.

Based on GAO's knowledge and recommendations from interviewees, GAO interviewed a non-probability, non-generalizable sample of 76 U.S. aviation industry stakeholders— including airlines, airports, labor unions, manufacturers, and general aviation—using a semi-structured format with closed and open-ended questions. GAO also discussed the perspectives with current FAA officials. The Department of Transportation provided technical comments on a draft of this product.

View GAO-14-770. For more information, contact Gerald Dillingham, Ph.D., at (202) 512-2834 or dillinghamg@gao.gov.

What GAO Found

The 76 aviation industry stakeholders with whom GAO spoke were generally positive regarding the Federal Aviation Administration's (FAA) operation of the current air traffic control (ATC) system but identified challenges about transitioning to the Next Generation Air Traffic Control System (NextGen). Specifically, the majority of stakeholders rated FAA as moderately to very capable of operating an efficient ATC system, but the majority also rated FAA as only marginally to moderately capable of implementing NextGen, FAA's initiative to modernize the system. Almost all (75) of the stakeholders identified challenges that they believe FAA faces, particularly in implementing the NextGen initiatives. These challenges included difficulty in (1) convincing reluctant aircraft owners to invest in the aircraft technology necessary to benefit from NextGen (46 stakeholders) and (2) mitigating the effects of an uncertain fiscal environment (43 stakeholders). FAA officials acknowledged and generally agreed with these challenges.

Sixty four stakeholders suggested a range of changes they believe could improve the efficiency of ATC operations and NextGen's implementation. The change stakeholders suggested most often was to modify how FAA's ATC operations and NextGen programs are funded, including the need to ensure that FAA has a predictable and long-term funding source. Other suggested changes were to improve human capital activities, such as air traffic controllers' training, and improve coordination with industry stakeholders. GAO has reported on these issues in the past, and in some cases, made recommendations, with which FAA concurred but has not yet implemented. GAO also asked stakeholders whether separating ATC services from FAA, such as the privatization of the ATC service provider, was an option; 27 of the stakeholders believed it was an option; another 26 believed it was an option, but had significant reservations about such a change. Support for this option was mixed among categories of stakeholders (see table below). Stakeholders identified several issues that would need to be taken into account before making any changes to the provision of ATC services, including lessons learned from other countries, funding sources for such a system, and the extent of Congress's role in overseeing a separate ATC system.

Stakeholder Responses to Whether Separating the Safety Regulator and the Air Traffic Control-Provider Functions into Separate Units or Organizations Is an Option

Industry category (number of stakeholders in category)	Yes	Maybe[a]	No	No opinion	No answer given
Airlines (17)	9	5	1	2	0
Airports (7)	1	3	2	1	0
Aviation experts and other relevant organizations (18)	10	6	2	0	0
General aviation (4)	1	1	1	0	1
Labor unions and professional associations (8)	1	3	2	2	0
Manufacturers and service providers (16)	4	5	3	4	0
Other stakeholders[b] (6)	1	3	1	0	1
Total	27	26	12	9	2

Source: GAO Analysis. | GAO-14-770

[a]Maybe represents stakeholders who qualified their "Yes" responses with significant reservations.
[b]Included in this other category are three industry categories with fewer than four stakeholders—Research & Development Organizations, Other Federal Agencies, and Passenger and Safety Groups.

_____ **United States Government Accountability Office**

Contents

Letter		1
	Background	3
	Industry Stakeholders Were Generally Positive Regarding the Performance of the Current ATC System but Cited Challenges to Transitioning to a Modernized System	10
	Industry Stakeholders Suggested Changes That Could Improve ATC System Performance and Modernization and Identified Issues to Be Considered If ATC Operations Were Separated from FAA	21
	Agency Comments	30
Appendix I	Objectives, Scope, and Methodology	31
Appendix II	List of the 76 Aviation Industry Stakeholders GAO Interviewed	34
Appendix III	Responses to GAO's Closed-Ended Question on Safety	37
Appendix IV	List of Challenges FAA Faces in Improving the Efficiency of the Air Traffic Control (ATC) System and Implementing NextGen, as Raised by the 76 Aviation Industry Stakeholders GAO Interviewed	38
Appendix V	List of Changes to FAA to Improve the Efficiency of the Air Traffic Control (ATC) System or the Implementation of NextGen, or Both, as Cited by the 76 Aviation Industry Stakeholders GAO Interviewed	40
Appendix VI	GAO Contact and Staff Acknowledgments	41
Related GAO Products		42

Tables

Table 1: Stakeholder Responses to GAO's Questions on Air Traffic Control (ATC) System's Efficiency and NextGen Implementation 11

Table 2: Stakeholder Responses to GAO Question on Separating Air Traffic Control (ATC) Services from Federal Aviation Administration (FAA) by Industry Category 27

Figures

Figure 1: Federal Aviation Administration's (FAA) Current Organizational Structure 4

Figure 2: Federal Aviation Administration's (FAA) Fiscal Year 2013 Congressional Appropriations by Account 5

Figure 3: Improvements to Phases of Flight Expected under NextGen 8

Figure 4: Procedures Using Conventional Equipment and Performance Based Navigation (PBN) Technologies 17

Figure 5: Very High Frequency Omnidirectional Radio Range (VOR) Station 21

Abbreviations

ADS-B	Automatic Dependent Surveillance-Broadcast
ANSP	air navigation service provider
ATC	air traffic control
ATO	Air Traffic Organization
CEO	chief executive officer
COO	chief operating officer
CANSO	Civil Air Navigation Services Organisation
EUROCONTROL	European Organisation for the Safety of Air Navigation
FAA	Federal Aviation Administration
IFR	instrument flight rules
NAC	NextGen Advisory Committee
NAS	National Airspace System
NAV Lean	Navigation Lean
NextGen	Next Generation Air Transportation System
OAPM	Optimization of Airspace and Procedures in the Metroplex
PBN	Performance Based Navigation
PMO	Program Management Office
RNAV	Area Navigation
RNP	Required Navigation Performance
VOR	Very High Frequency Omnidirectional Radio Range

GAO
U.S. GOVERNMENT ACCOUNTABILITY OFFICE

441 G St. N.W.
Washington, DC 20548

September 12, 2014

The Honorable Bill Shuster,
Chairman
The Honorable Nick J. Rahall, II
Ranking Member
Committee on Transportation and Infrastructure
House of Representatives

The Honorable Frank A. LoBiondo
Chairman
The Honorable Rick Larsen
Ranking Member
Subcommittee on Aviation
Committee on Transportation and Infrastructure
House of Representatives

The U.S. National Airspace System (NAS) handles over 50,000 flights a day and more than 700 million passengers each year and is generally considered not only the busiest and most complex air traffic control system in the world but also the safest. Key aviation stakeholders— the Federal Aviation Administration (FAA), airlines, airports, aircraft manufacturers, and the National Transportation Safety Board—work together to ensure these results. However, over the past two decades, U.S. aviation stakeholders have debated whether the FAA should be the entity in the United States that operates and modernizes the air traffic control (ATC) system. Since its inception in 1958, FAA has overseen the entire NAS, owning and operating the ATC system and regulating industry safety, aircraft, and operations. In 1995, Congress considered reforming FAA in response to government and industry frustration with the agency's slow pace in modernizing the ATC system and concerns about constrained spending for aviation due to efforts to reduce the budget deficit. Similar conditions exist today: the recent constrained fiscal environment has forced federal agencies—including FAA—to cut their spending through budget sequestration and employee furloughs. At the same time, the current ATC system continues to use aging technologies and infrastructure—such as analog communications and ground-based radar—and FAA continues to face challenges modernizing the ATC system through its Next Generation Air Transportation System (NextGen) initiative. These conditions have rekindled industry debate about whether (1) organizational changes need to be made within FAA and (2) alternative NAS structures—such as making FAA an independent agency or commercializing ATC services—could provide ATC services, as well as modernize the ATC system, more efficiently.

You requested that we gather U.S. aviation industry views on FAA's ATC system operations and modernization. This report examines the perspectives of a wide range of aviation stakeholders on:

- the performance of the current ATC system and its modernization through the NextGen initiative, and any challenges FAA may face in managing these activities, and
- potential changes, if any, that could improve the performance of the ATC system, including FAA's modernization initiative.

To perform this work, we interviewed a non-probability sample of 76 aviation industry stakeholders from a cross-section of the industry. We selected stakeholders based on our knowledge of the industry and recommendations from interviewees. We wanted to obtain perspectives from individuals and organizations with direct experience, as users, or knowledge, through research or study, of the current ATC system, modernization efforts, and FAA's management of the system. As such, we limited our review to U.S.-based companies and airlines and sought the views of individuals and organizations with a stake in the performance of the NAS. The selected stakeholders represented the following industry sectors: airlines, airports, aviation experts and other relevant organizations, general aviation, labor unions and professional associations, manufacturers and service providers, other federal government agencies—the Department of Defense and National Aeronautics and Space Administration, passenger and safety groups, and research and development organizations.

To obtain stakeholder perspectives, we used a semi-structured interview format with both closed- and open-ended questions. The intent of our open-ended questions was to engage the stakeholders in a conversation about the issues they considered most important and relevant. To determine the common themes that we are reporting on, we conducted a content analysis of each of the interviewees' responses. The numbers reported for our open-ended questions represent those stakeholders who, during our interviews, raised a challenge or issue to consider or suggested a change. It does not mean that the remaining stakeholders agreed or disagreed with that challenge, change, or issue. In our discussion of stakeholder views obtained through our open-ended questions, we aggregated their responses and reported on stakeholders perspectives in general. The results of our review are not generalizable to the industry as a whole.

We also interviewed the following FAA senior management officials on their perspectives and reactions to our preliminary results on stakeholder perspectives: Administrator; Deputy Administrator/Chief NextGen Officer; Assistant Administrator for NextGen; Associate Administrator for Aviation Safety; Chief Operating Officer (COO) of the Air Traffic Organization (ATO); and the Assistant Administrator for Policy, International Affairs, and Environment. Finally, we reviewed GAO reports that were related to stakeholder-identified themes, including collaboration with stakeholders, delivery of NextGen capabilities, and Performance Based Navigation procedures, and FAA leadership in overseeing NextGen implementation. Appendix I describes our objectives, scope, and methodology in greater detail. See also appendix II for the complete list of stakeholders we interviewed.

In addition, you asked us to obtain stakeholders' perspectives on the safety of the NAS. Nearly all of the stakeholders we interviewed agreed that the NAS is extremely or very safe. (See app. III for stakeholders' ratings of the safety of the NAS.) For this reason, we focused this report on the stakeholders' perspectives on ATC operations and NextGen modernization and changes that could improve FAA's efforts in these areas.

We conducted this performance audit from November 2013 to September 2014, in accordance with generally accepted government auditing standards. Those standards require that we plan and perform the audit to obtain sufficient, appropriate evidence to provide a reasonable basis for our findings and conclusions based on our audit objectives. We believe that the evidence obtained provides a reasonable basis for our findings and conclusions based on our audit objectives.

Background

FAA's primary mission is to provide the safest, most efficient aerospace system in the world. FAA oversees operating and maintaining this system, known as the NAS, as well as the safety of aircraft and operators. FAA operates and maintains the NAS through the following:

- a workforce of technicians, air traffic controllers, and other staff who work in airport towers, terminal areas, en-route centers, oceanic air traffic control centers, and other facilities, and

- the ATC and other supporting systems and infrastructure, including ground-based surveillance radar facilities, communication equipment, automation systems, and the facilities that house and support these systems.

Various offices within FAA are responsible for the air traffic control system and its modernization through the NextGen initiative. The ATO, headed by the COO, is responsible for the day-to-day operations and maintenance of the air traffic control system. The NextGen Office, ATO, and Office of Aviation Safety are involved with various aspects of NextGen's management and implementation. The Office of Airports is responsible for all programs related to airport safety and inspections, standards for airport design, construction, and operation. In this role, the Office of Airports supports the implementation of NextGen. These offices report to the Deputy Administrator, who also has the designation Chief NextGen Officer (see fig. 1).

Figure 1: Federal Aviation Administration's (FAA) Current Organizational Structure

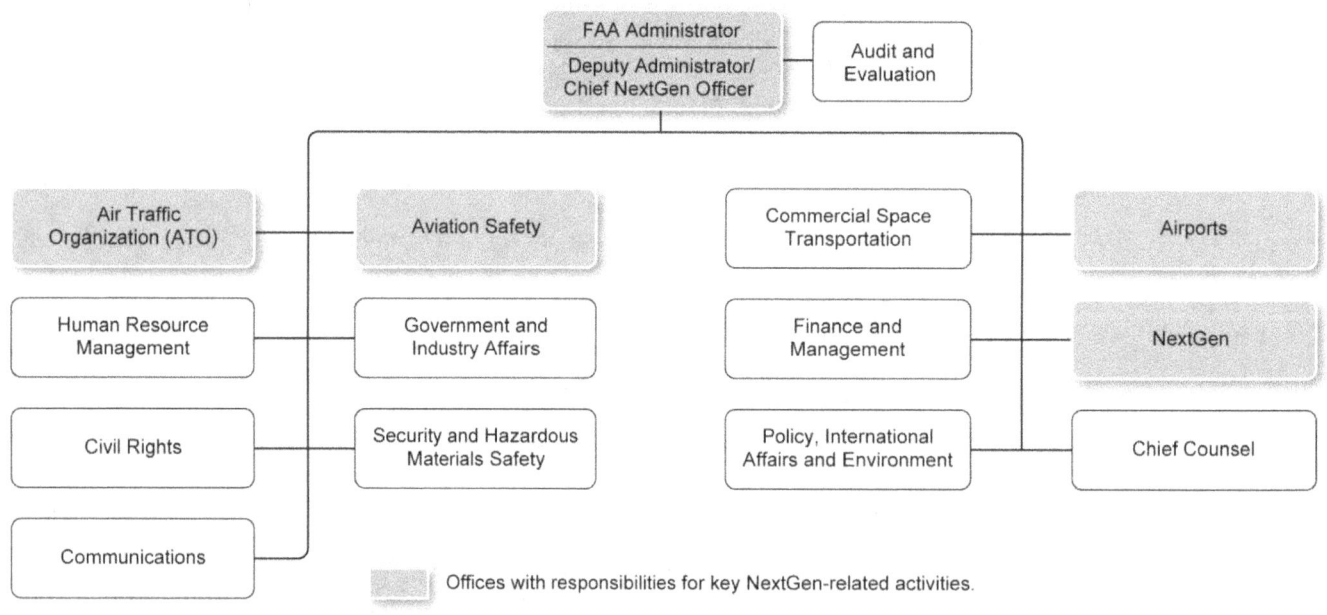

Sources: FAA and GAO. | GAO-14-770

FAA receives funds annually through congressional appropriations into four accounts:

- The operations account funds, among other things, the operation and maintenance of the air traffic control system.

GAO-14-770 Air Traffic Control System

- The facilities and equipment account funds technological improvements to the air traffic control system, including NextGen.
- The research, engineering, and development account funds research on issues related to aviation safety and NextGen systems.
- The Airport Improvement Program account provides grants for airport planning and development.

See figure 2 for percentage of fiscal year 2013 congressional appropriations by account.

Figure 2: Federal Aviation Administration's (FAA) Fiscal Year 2013 Congressional Appropriations by Account

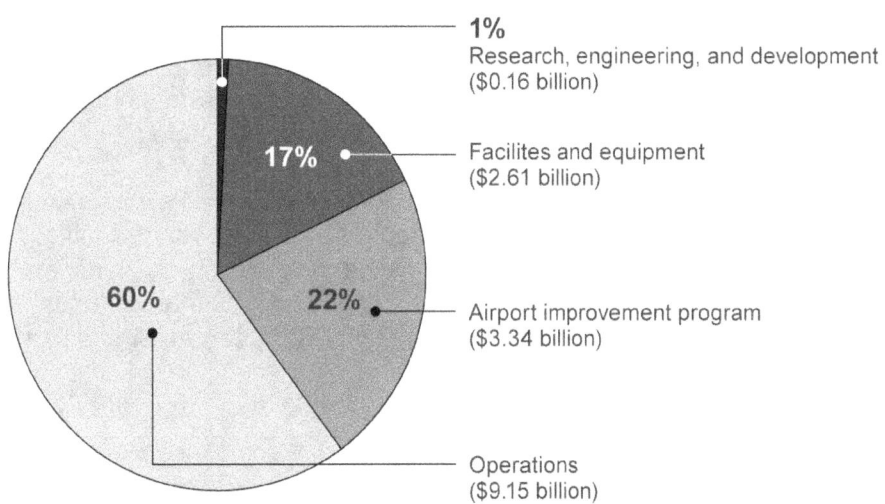

1%
Research, engineering, and development
($0.16 billion)

Facilites and equipment
($2.61 billion)

Airport improvement program
($3.34 billion)

Operations
($9.15 billion)

Sources: FAA Budget Estimates Fiscal Year 2015 and U.S. Department of Transportation. | GA0-14-770

Congress appropriates funding from the Airport and Airway Trust Fund, which receives revenues from a series of excise taxes paid by users of the national airspace system, as well as from general revenues. The Trust Fund provides nearly all of the funding for FAA's capital investments in the airport and airway system. Revenue sources for the trust fund include passenger ticket taxes, segment taxes, air cargo taxes, and taxes paid by both commercial and general aviation aircraft. The trust fund also provides a substantial portion of funding for operations—for example 80 percent of FAA's $15.9-billion funding in fiscal year 2014. The remaining amount was appropriated from general revenues.

GAO-14-770 Air Traffic Control System

The U.S. Air Traffic Control System versus International Air Traffic Control Systems

Whereas FAA operates, maintains, and regulates the air traffic control system in the United States, in countries such as the United Kingdom, Germany, and Canada, their air navigation service providers (ANSP) are commercialized and handle the day-to-day operations of the air traffic control systems, while the governments regulate these activities. These ANSPs employ the workforce, maintain the infrastructure, and undertake modernization efforts. International ANSPs vary in the extent of government ownership and commercialization, with some as state-owned corporations, some as public-private partnerships, and some as private corporations.[1]

According to two recent international analyses comparing ANSPs from different countries on a range of performance measures including productivity, efficiency, and cost-effectiveness, FAA operates one of the most efficient ATC systems. According to a 2012 comparison of air traffic management performance between FAA and the combined 37 ANSPs of Europe,[2] the United States had a similar arrival punctuality rate with Europe for a similar amount of continental airspace. Another international comparison, completed in 2013, of performance data from FAA and 22 global ANSPs showed similar results, with FAA ranking second in productivity.[3,4] However, it is difficult to compare performance, as air spaces are different. For example, FAA's ATC system controls about 60 percent more flights than Europe,[5] its airspace is nearly twice as dense as that of the European ANSPs, and it has 23 percent fewer air traffic

---

[1]GAO, *Air Traffic Control: Characteristics and Performance of Selected International Air Navigation Service Providers and Lessons Learned from Their Commercialization,* GAO-05-769 (Washington, D.C.: July 29, 2005).

[2]*Comparison of Air Traffic Management-Related Performance: U.S. – Europe, Final Report.* Produced by the European Organisation for the Safety of Air Navigation (EUROCONTROL) Performance Review Commission and FAA's Air Traffic Organization, November 2013. © Air Traffic Organization System Operations Services (FAA) © European Organisation for the Safety of Air Navigation (EUROCONTROL).

[3]Civil Air Navigation Services Organisation (CANSO), *Global Air Navigation Services Performance Report 2013: 2008-2012 ANSP Performance Results* (January 2014).

[4]Productivity was measured by the number of hours flown under instrument flight rules (IFR) per air traffic controller. Canada's NAV CANADA was ranked first in 2012 with 1,739 IFR flight hours per controller to FAA's 1,729.

[5]This comparison includes only those flights operating under instrumental flight rules, a set of rules governing the conduct of flight under instrument meteorological conditions, including bad weather.

controllers. In addition, Europe has to coordinate among 37 ANSPs, while the United States has one.

Air Traffic Control Modernization

Although FAA is recognized for safety and relative efficiency, its attempts to modernize the ATC system have been less successful. We have chronicled the difficulties FAA has faced completing what it envisioned initially in 1981 as a 10-year program to upgrade and replace NAS facilities and equipment.[6] For example, in August 1995, we found substantial cost and schedule overruns.[7] To address these difficulties, in the past, Congress gave FAA acquisition and human capital flexibilities to improve the agency's management of the modernization program. Specifically, in 1995, Congress directed FAA to implement new acquisition and personnel management systems and exempted the agency from certain federal acquisition and personnel laws and rules.[8] In June 2005, we found that FAA had largely implemented these flexibilities.[9]

However, modernization difficulties persisted, and Congress directed FAA in 2003 to conceptualize and plan NextGen.[10] NextGen was envisioned at that time as a major redesign of the air transportation system to increase

---

[6]For example, see GAO, *Transportation: DOT Should Terminate Further LORAN-C Development and Modernization and Exploit the Potential of the NAVSTAR/Global Positioning System,* MASAD-81-42 (Washington, D.C.: Sep. 18, 1981); *Transportation: Delays in Critical Air Traffic Control Modernization Projects Require Increased FAA Attention to Existing Systems,* T-IMTEC-91-14 (Washington, D.C.: Jun. 14, 1991); *Air Traffic Control: FAA's Modernization Efforts – Past, Present, and Future,* GAO-04-227T (Washington, D.C.: Oct. 30, 2003); and *Next Generation Air Transportation System: Progress and Challenges Associated with the Transformation of the National Airspace System,* GAO-07-25 (Washington, D.C.: Dec. 13, 2006). For a list of our more recent findings on FAA's modernization efforts, see Related GAO Products at the end of this report.

[7]For example, see GAO, *Federal Aviation Administration: Issues Related to FAA Reform,* GAO/T-RCED-95-247 (Washington, D.C.: Aug. 2, 1995).

[8]Department of Transportation and Related Agencies Appropriations Act, Pub. L. 104-50, §§ 347, 348, 109 Stat. 436, 460 (1995).

[9]GAO, *National Airspace System: FAA Has Made Progress but Continues to Face Challenges in Acquiring Major Air Traffic control Systems,* GAO-05-331 (Washington, D.C.: June 10, 2005).

[10] Vision 100—Century of Aviation Reauthorization Act, Pub. L. No. 108-176, § 709, 117 Stat. 2490, 2582-2585 (2003).

efficiency, enhance safety, and reduce flight delays. NextGen is planned to incorporate precision satellite navigation and surveillance; digital, networked communications; an integrated weather system; and more. This complex undertaking requires acquiring new integrated air traffic control systems; developing new flight procedures, standards, and regulations; and creating and maintaining new supporting infrastructure. This transformation is designed to dramatically change the roles and responsibilities of both air traffic controllers and pilots and change the way they interface with their systems. The involvement of airlines and other aviation stakeholders is also critical, since full implementation of NextGen will necessitate airlines and others to invest in new avionics and other technologies to take advantage of NextGen technologies. See figure 3 for the expected benefits from NextGen implementation as depicted through improvements to the phases of flight.

Figure 3: Improvements to Phases of Flight Expected under NextGen

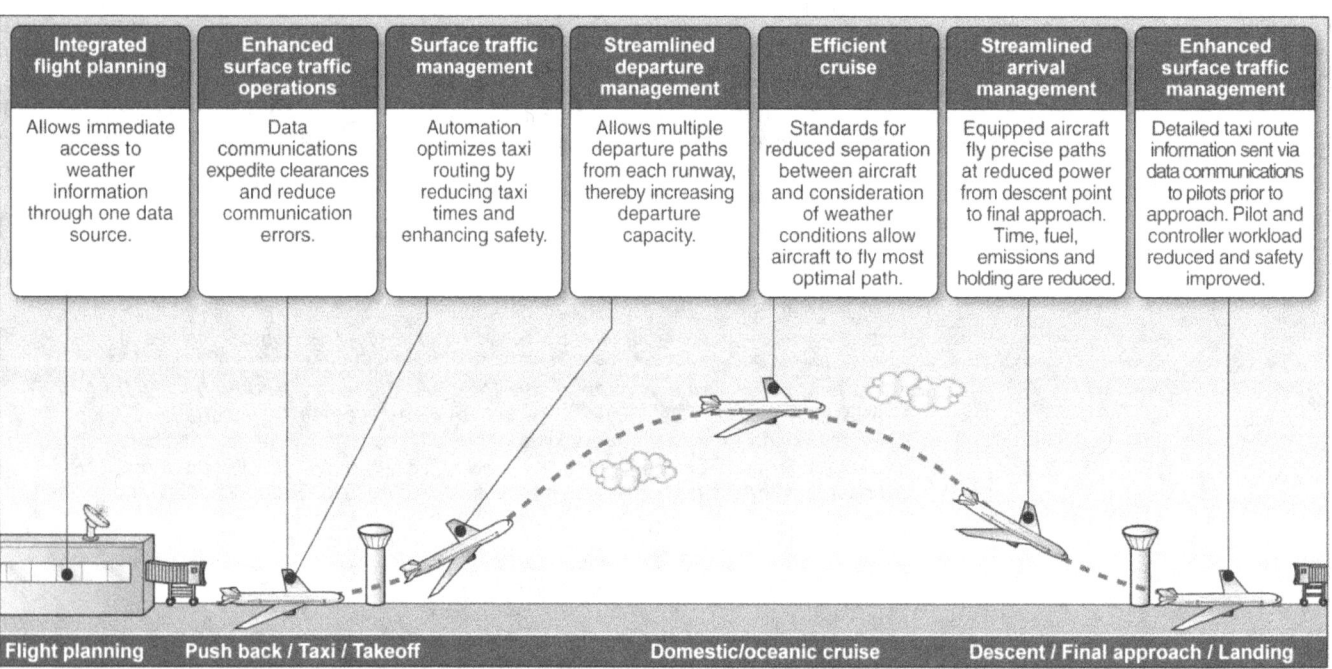

Integrated flight planning	Enhanced surface traffic operations	Surface traffic management	Streamlined departure management	Efficient cruise	Streamlined arrival management	Enhanced surface traffic management
Allows immediate access to weather information through one data source.	Data communications expedite clearances and reduce communication errors.	Automation optimizes taxi routing by reducing taxi times and enhancing safety.	Allows multiple departure paths from each runway, thereby increasing departure capacity.	Standards for reduced separation between aircraft and consideration of weather conditions allow aircraft to fly most optimal path.	Equipped aircraft fly precise paths at reduced power from descent point to final approach. Time, fuel, emissions and holding are reduced.	Detailed taxi route information sent via data communications to pilots prior to approach. Pilot and controller workload reduced and safety improved.

Flight planning   Push back / Taxi / Takeoff   Domestic/oceanic cruise   Descent / Final approach / Landing

Source: GAO analysis of FAA information. | GA0-14-770

In addition, to address stakeholder and congressional concerns over NextGen management practices and the pace of modernization efforts over the last decade, FAA has reorganized several times. These changes included:

- In 2003, FAA hired a COO and in 2004 created the ATO to transform the air traffic control system into a more performance-based organization and improve the modernization effort.

- In 2011, FAA moved the office responsible for coordinating NextGen activities—the NextGen Office—out of the ATO and made it report directly to the Deputy Administrator to increase NextGen's visibility within and outside of the agency and create a direct line of authority for NextGen.

- In 2012, FAA created the Program Management Office (PMO), within the ATO, to improve the oversight of ATO's acquisition and implementation efforts, including those for NextGen.

- At the direction of the FAA Modernization and Reform Act of 2012, FAA created the Chief NextGen Officer position, currently held by the Deputy FAA Administrator, who reports directly to the FAA Administrator.[11]

However, challenges continue to persist, as we found in April 2013, August 2013, and February 2014.[12] Specifically, we found that while FAA had made some progress in implementing the NextGen modernization program, FAA continued to experience challenges, including in the following areas:

- *Human capital activities*: Improving and sustaining NextGen leadership and preparing FAA's workforce.
- *Program management*: Prioritizing projects to achieve some near-and mid-term benefits and managing NextGen interdependencies.

---

[11]Pub. L. No. 112–95, §204, 126 Stat. 11, 37 (2012).

[12]GAO, *NextGen Air Transportation System: FAA Has Made Some Progress in Midterm Implementation, but Ongoing Challenges Limit Expected Benefits*, GAO-13-264 (Washington, D.C.: Apr. 8, 2013); *National Airspace System: Improved Budgeting Could Help FAA Better Determine Future Operations and Maintenance Priorities*, GAO-13-693 (Washington, D.C.: Aug. 22, 2013); and *FAA Reauthorization Act: Progress and Challenges Implementing Various Provisions of the 2012 Act*, GAO-14-285T (Washington, D.C.: Feb. 5, 2014). In this report, we made five recommendations to FAA regarding aspects of performance-based navigation implementation as well as coordinating and communicating with appropriate stakeholders. As of the writing of this report, all of these recommendations remained open.

- *Coordination with industry stakeholders*: Gaining greater involvement from industry stakeholders in FAA's initiatives and equipping aircraft with NextGen technologies.
- *Transitioning to NextGen*: Balancing the needs of the current ATC system and NextGen and consolidating and realigning FAA's facilities.

In these reports, we made six recommendations to FAA regarding the improvement of budget planning, performance-based navigation implementation, and stakeholder coordination and communication. DOT concurred with these recommendations, but as of August 2014, had not yet implemented them.

Industry Stakeholders Were Generally Positive Regarding the Performance of the Current ATC System but Cited Challenges to Transitioning to a Modernized System

Stakeholders Said that the United States' Current ATC System is Efficient, whereas NextGen Has Experienced Difficulties

Stakeholders' views on FAA's capability to operate an efficient ATC system generally align with the two international analyses described previously. Almost three-quarters (53) of the 72 stakeholders who provided a rating rated FAA as moderately to very able to operate an efficient ATC system. Four stakeholders did not rate FAA on this issue. (See table 1 for the stakeholders' ratings.) In addition, during our interviews, over three times as many of the stakeholders specifically mentioned that the ATC system is generally efficient (37) than those who said the system is not (12). Fourteen stakeholders specifically said that FAA operates the most efficient system in the world. Notwithstanding this generally positive assessment, stakeholders raised areas where FAA could improve. For example, 29 stakeholders indicated that FAA does not handle irregular air traffic operations very well, such as those caused by inclement weather.

Stakeholders' views regarding NextGen implementation also reflect our past findings on FAA's difficulties in implementing the initiative. Eighty percent (56) of the 70 stakeholders who provided a rating rated FAA as marginally to moderately able to implement NextGen. Six stakeholders did not rate FAA. (See table 1.) In addition, during our interviews, more than three times as many of the stakeholders (43) said that FAA's overall implementation of NextGen was not going well than those who said it was going well (13), and 30 specifically mentioned that FAA was not doing well managing technology programs in general and NextGen acquisitions and contracts in particular.

Table 1: Stakeholder Responses to GAO's Questions on Air Traffic Control (ATC) System's Efficiency and NextGen Implementation

How would you characterize the level of capability Federal Aviation Administration has shown in:

Capability rating	Operating an efficient ATC system? Number of stakeholder responses	Implementing NextGen?
Extremely	8	1
Between very to extremely[a]	3	0
Very	19	6
Between moderately to very[a]	7	2
Moderately	27	26
Between marginally to moderately[a]	3	8
Marginally	2	22
Between not at all to marginally[a]	0	3
Not at all	3	2
No rating given	4	6
Total	**76**	**76**

Source: GAO Analysis. | GAO-14-770

[a]This rating was not given to the stakeholders as a choice; however, the stakeholders' answers fell between these categories.

In our interviews with FAA senior management, officials acknowledged that stakeholders' complaints about NextGen were not new. They also said that the agency is taking steps to improve implementation, that NextGen is now on track and that the agency is starting to focus more on using these technologies to improve flight efficiencies and reduce flight time and fuel use, steps and a focus that should result in stakeholders realizing tangible benefits in the future.

Stakeholders Identified Challenges Related to Overcoming NextGen Implementation Difficulties

Almost all (75) of the 76 stakeholders identified challenges that they stated FAA faces in improving ATC operations and overcoming difficulties in implementing NextGen. (See app. IV for a list and description of the challenges for FAA that stakeholders identified during our interviews.) The six challenges stakeholders noted most often are discussed below. These challenges are long-standing, as we have issued reports on them as far back as the 1980s, and more recently in the past few years.

Ensuring Aircraft Are Equipped to Take Advantage of NextGen

Consistent with what we have found in the past, stakeholders and FAA officials told us that ensuring that aircraft are equipped with avionics to take advantage of NextGen technologies is a challenge. Full implementation of NextGen will necessitate that system users make significant investment in new technologies. FAA estimated in 2013 that, of the estimated $18.1-billion overall implementation cost that is to be shared between airlines and FAA, airlines would need to invest $6.6 billion on avionics to realize the full potential benefits from NextGen capabilities.[13] Forty-six of the stakeholders we interviewed raised this issue as a challenge for FAA, such as in convincing users to equip their aircraft with avionics to take advantage of NextGen technologies. Stakeholders explained that users have been reluctant to equip their aircraft due to the expense and uncertainty over FAA's ability to meet timelines for deploying NextGen technologies. In April 2013, we found that airlines and other stakeholders had expressed skepticism about the progress FAA had made to date in implementing NextGen technologies, skepticism that, in turn, had affected their confidence about whether benefits would justify these investments.[14] While some stakeholders agreed that equipping aircraft is necessary for successful and continuous modernization, they differed in who bore responsibility for paying for equipage—users or FAA. In August 2013,[15] we noted that the 2012 FAA Modernization and Reform Act[16] required FAA to report on options to encourage equipping aircraft with NextGen technologies and the costs and benefits of each option. FAA officials we interviewed said that they

Automatic Dependent Surveillance-Broadcast (ADS-B)

ADS-B, a key NextGen program, is a technology that enables aircraft to continually broadcast flight data—such as position, air speed, and altitude, among other types of information—to air traffic controllers and other aircraft.

- ADS-B Out is the ability to transmit ADS-B signals.
- ADS-B In is the ability to receive ADS-B signals from the ground and other aircraft, process those signals, and display traffic and weather information to flight crews.

The Federal Aviation Administration required that airplanes be equipped with *ADS-B Out* by January 1, 2020. On the other hand, aircraft operators are not required to install *ADS-B In*, but may choose to do so, as is the case for most NextGen equipment.

Source: GAO. | GAO-14-770.

---

[13]These estimates were in 2011 dollars and reflected total expenditures on NextGen midterm improvements from 2007 through 2018. These estimates included equipping aircraft with the Required Navigation Performance (RNP) package, as well as other NextGen technologies.

[14]GAO-13-264.

[15]GAO-13-693.

[16]Pub. L. No. 112–95, §§ 211(c), 222, 126 Stat. 46, 54 (2012).

have completed the installation of the ground infrastructure for Automatic Dependent Surveillance-Broadcast (ADS-B) Out and that aviation system users, in turn, must equip their aircraft with ADS-B Out avionics by the FAA's 2020 equipage deadline.

Mitigating the Effects of an Uncertain Fiscal Environment

Both the aviation stakeholders and FAA officials we interviewed regard budget uncertainty as a challenge for FAA. Forty-three stakeholders raised budget uncertainty as a difficulty for FAA's ability to continue operation of an efficient ATC system and/or implementation of NextGen. One factor stakeholders raised as contributing to budget uncertainties is the annual appropriations process. In all but 3 of the last 30 years, Congress has passed "continuing resolutions" to provide funding for agencies to continue operating until agreement is reached on final appropriations.[17] Further, according to the House Transportation and Infrastructure Committee, prior to the FAA Modernization and Reform Act of 2012, FAA had operated under 22 extensions, that provided short-term funding for the agency since the expiration of the 2007 Aviation Authorization legislation. According to some stakeholders, the stops and starts associated with continuing resolutions make it difficult for FAA to carry out long-term planning and strategic development of future technologies and innovation.[18] We found in September 2009 and March 2013 that continuing resolutions can create budget uncertainty for agencies about both when they will receive their final appropriation and what level of funding will ultimately be available.[19] We further found that operating under continuing resolutions can also complicate agency operations and cause inefficiencies, such as leading to repetitive work, limiting agencies' decision-making options, and making trade-offs more difficult. On the other hand, attempting to mitigate the effects of an unpredictable funding stream is not a new challenge for FAA, or for many

---

[17]GAO-13-464T.

[18]A "continuing resolution" is an appropriation act that provides budget authority for federal agencies, specific activities, or both to continue in operation when Congress and the President have not completed action on the regular appropriation acts by the beginning of the fiscal year.

[19]GAO, *Continuing Resolutions: Uncertainty Limited Management Options and Increased Workload in Selected Agencies*, GAO-09-879 (Washington, D.C.: Sept. 24, 2009); and *Budget Issues: Effects of Budget Uncertainty from Continuing Resolutions on Agency Operations*, GAO-13-464T (Washington, D.C.: Mar. 13, 2013).

other federal agencies that have had to operate in times of an uncertain fiscal environment.[20]

Stakeholders also indicated that the current budgetary conditions—the fiscal year 2013 budget sequestration[21] (the across-the-board cancellation of budgetary resources) along with the associated employee furloughs and the October 2013 government shutdown—have made FAA's funding less predictable. In turn, this can make it difficult for FAA to run a 24/7 operation and maintain the ATC system as part of the transition to NextGen. In March 2014, we detailed the effects of the fiscal year 2013 budget sequestration on federal agencies, including FAA, such as reducing or delaying some public services and disrupting some operations.[22] We found that the DOT took actions to minimize the effects of sequestration on FAA operations by beginning to plan for it during the summer of 2012, focusing on ensuring the safety of the traveling public, according to DOT officials.[23] DOT halted these actions when it was provided with statutory authority to make a one-time transfer of $253 million between budget accounts to address these issues. As a result of this transfer, FAA minimized the number of planned furlough days and restored ATC services and other aviation activities; however, these efforts did not prevent delays from occurring in major metropolitan areas—including New York, Chicago, and Southern California—according to FAA, because fewer controllers were available to manage air traffic.

FAA senior management generally agreed with the stakeholders' perspective that unpredictable budgets make planning and managing the ATC system and NextGen programs difficult and result in delays and inefficiencies. The senior managers did not offer specific solutions; however, they indicated that if FAA received more funding that was available across fiscal years, rather than just for one fiscal year at a

---

[20]GAO-13-464T, GAO, *2013 Sequestration: Agencies Reduced Some Services and Investments, While Taking Certain Actions to Mitigate Effects*, GAO-14-244 (Washington, D.C.: Mar. 6, 2014).

[21]GAO-14-244.

[22]GAO-14-244.

[23]Planning included determining the number of furlough days for FAA air traffic controllers and other employees and identifying federal contract air traffic control towers for closure.

time,[24] and had a greater ability to move funds between accounts, FAA would be able to improve its operations and NextGen implementation.

Improving Human Capital Activities to Meet Future NextGen and Operational Requirements

Consistent with what we have found in the past, the stakeholders and FAA senior management agree that improving human capital activities is a challenge for FAA. Forty-two stakeholders identified human capital activities as a challenge for FAA in improving the efficiency of the ATC systems and/or implementing NextGen. Among the human capital challenges the stakeholders identified were matching workforce skills with FAA needs for hiring and staffing, insufficient training, and planning for upcoming retirements. FAA senior management also raised human capital challenges during our discussions with them. For example, one senior official acknowledged that providing required training is an element of delivering the full capability of NextGen and is a challenge but that FAA was working to address this challenge.

We have also reported on FAA's workforce training and staffing issues in the past. For example, in August 2013 we found that FAA had been working to address long-standing challenges associated with involving its air traffic controller and technician workforce in developing and implementing NextGen systems, steps that are critical to the successful implementation of NextGen. In addition, we found that during the NextGen transition, FAA would need a sufficient number of skilled controllers who are able to increasingly rely on automation, technicians who are able to properly maintain and certify both existing and NextGen systems, and a sufficient acquisitions workforce to successfully acquire NextGen systems and equipment.[25]

Implementing New Navigation Procedures

Stakeholders identified challenges in implementing new navigation procedures, and we have found similar challenges in previous work. A large percentage of the current U.S. air carrier fleet is equipped to fly using Performance Based Navigation (PBN) procedures, which are precise routes that use the Global Positioning System or glide descent paths (see fig. 4). While 21 stakeholders said the development and implementation of PBN-related procedures was improving or working well, almost twice as many, or 41, of the stakeholders said that this

---

[24]Congress can appropriate funds to federal agencies that are available for a specified fiscal year, for multiple fiscal years, or that remain available for an indefinite period of time.

[25]GAO-13-693.

Performance Based Navigation (PBN)

PBN procedures use satellite-based guidance to route aircraft and improve approaches at airports. There are two main types of PBN procedures, Area Navigation (RNAV) and Required Navigation Performance (RNP), which vary in the level of precision guidance they can provide.

Over the longer term, PBN procedures are intended to offer airlines more time- and cost-efficient approaches to airports. In the near term, during the transition period to full implementation of NextGen technologies, benefits include fuel savings and increased efficiency, particularly in congested airspace.

As the Federal Aviation Administration's primary effort to implement new PBN procedures, the Optimization of Airspace and Procedures in the Metroplex initiative focuses on priority metroplexes with airport operations that have a large effect on the overall efficiency of the National Airspace System.

FAA updated its plans and, as of June 2014, there are 10 metroplexes, of which the Houston metroplex project has been implemented with one more metroplex scheduled for implementation by the end of 2014.

Source: GAO. | GAO-14-770.

process was not working well or moving too slowly. Even when stakeholders said that there have been some things working well, such as successes like the Greener Skies Over Seattle initiative—a satellite-based navigation arrival procedure intended to save aviation system users more than two million gallons of fuel a year and significantly reduce aircraft exhaust and emissions—they pointed to other areas where implementation is taking too long. In April 2013, we found that FAA continues to face challenges in implementing PBN procedures and in explaining to stakeholders the benefits that accrue from their use. Specifically, FAA is not fully leveraging its ability to streamline the development of PBN procedures and the use of third parties to develop, test, and maintain these flight procedures.[26]

Senior FAA officials emphasized that their Optimization of Airspace and Procedures in the Metroplex (OAPM) initiative[27] is yielding good results and pointed to the successful use of PBN procedures not only in Seattle but also in the areas around Houston,[28] North Texas, Washington, D.C., and Denver. Officials also said that implementing PBN is one of their top priorities and is part of an effort to deliver near term-benefits and capabilities to system users by 2016. Officials explained that they are working on PBN, through several metroplex-based initiatives, and all parts of the country will not see PBN benefits at the same time.

---

[26]GAO-13-264, GAO-14-285T.

[27]OAPM is most currently referred to as "Metroplex," according to FAA.

[28]On June 18, 2014, FAA announced the successful implementation of the airspace redesign project as part of the OAPM initiative in the Houston metroplex. FAA expects this redesign to create more efficient routes, deliver more on-time flights, and reduce fuel consumption for those flying into and out of the Houston metroplex.

Figure 4: Procedures Using Conventional Equipment and Performance Based Navigation (PBN) Technologies

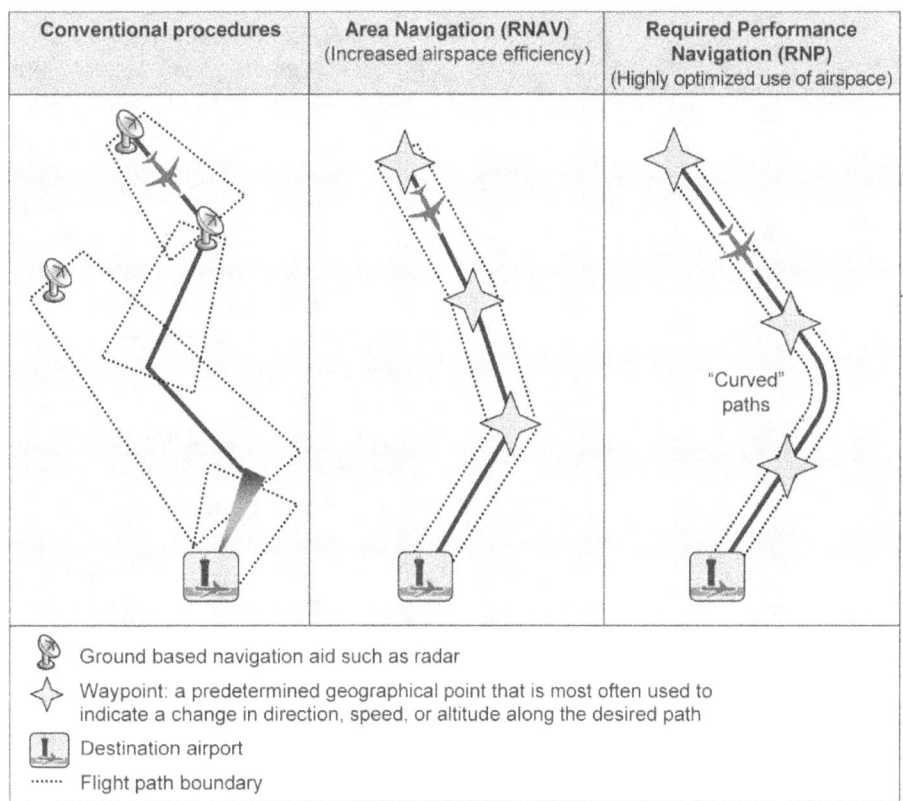

Conventional procedures	Area Navigation (RNAV) (Increased airspace efficiency)	Required Performance Navigation (RNP) (Highly optimized use of airspace)

"Curved" paths

Ground based navigation aid such as radar

Waypoint: a predetermined geographical point that is most often used to indicate a change in direction, speed, or altitude along the desired path

Destination airport

Flight path boundary

Sources: FAA and GAO. | GA0-14-770

Articulating What NextGen Is and Delivering Benefits in the Near Term

Consistent with what we have found in previous work, stakeholders told us that FAA needs to deliver benefits of NextGen in the near term. To convince aviation system users to make investments in NextGen equipment, FAA must continue to deliver systems, procedures, and capabilities that demonstrate near-term benefits and returns on users' investments.[29] Forty stakeholders identified as a challenge FAA's inability to articulate to the industry what NextGen is and what near-term benefits NextGen is going to provide to users. Similarly, in April 2013,[30] we noted

---

[29]GAO-14-285T.

[30]GAO-13-264. This report specifically mentioned the period of 2013-2018 for demonstrating benefits.

the need for FAA to demonstrate to stakeholders NextGen benefits over the next few years. For example, we found that FAA had made some progress in key operational improvement areas, such as upgrading airborne traffic management to enhance the flow of aircraft in congested airspace,[31] revising standards to enhance airport capacity,[32] and focusing FAA's PBN efforts at priority OAPM sites[33] with airport operations that have a large effect on the overall efficiency of the NAS. However, we also found that in pursuing these near-term benefits, FAA had to make trade-offs in selecting sites and did not fully integrate implementation of its operational improvement efforts at airports. We concluded that because of the interdependency of the improvements, their limited integration could also limit benefits in the near term. Accordingly, we recommended, among other things, that FAA should proactively identify new PBN procedures for the NAS, based on NextGen goals and targets, and evaluate external requests so that FAA can select appropriate solutions and implement guidelines for ensuring timely inclusion of operational improvements at metroplexes such as OAPMs. DOT concurred with these recommendations and is working to address them.

FAA senior managers said they were aware of stakeholders' desire for near-term benefits and told us that they either have taken or plan to take the following steps to address stakeholders' concerns.

- FAA plans to emphasize "high priorities" for users based on recommendations of two FAA advisory committees—the NextGen Advisory Committee (NAC) and the RTCA (once called the Radio

---

[31]We found that through 2018, FAA was focusing on updating its Traffic Management Advisor, an airborne arrival-sequencing program that assigns times when aircraft destined for the same airport should cross certain points in order to reach the destination airport at a specific time and in an efficient order.

[32]We found that FAA had recently approved a few revisions to existing standards, which should benefit a handful of airports in the midterm, but further revisions were required before the envisioned efficiency and capacity benefits of midterm NextGen improvements can be fully realized.

[33]A metroplex is a major airport or multi-airport airspace. The seven prioritized metroplex sites are Atlanta, Charlotte, Chicago, Dallas/Fort Worth, New York, Philadelphia, and Southern California.

Technical Commission for Aeronautics).[34] The high priorities are new multiple runway operational procedures at 7 airports by fiscal year 2015, PBN procedures at 9 metroplexes and an additional two metroplexes by October 2014, surface surveillance at 44 airports by fiscal year 2017, and data communications to provide tower clearance delivery at 57 airports by fiscal year 2016.

- FAA has identified seven NextGen and NextGen-related programs that will be able to deliver near-term benefits and capabilities by 2016, with no additional requirements for users to equip their aircraft until the January 1, 2020, FAA-required deadline for aircraft to be equipped with ADS-B Out technology.[35]
- The FAA Administrator has begun holding quarterly briefings on NextGen progress and benefits with airline chief executive officers (CEO); however, senior management noted that the diverse range of interests within the industry, and even between CEOs and operations staff within the same company, can make the communication of NextGen progress and benefits challenging.
- According to FAA's Assistant Administrator for NextGen, in October 2014 FAA will release a road map outlining the official timeline of the implementation of its NextGen modernization project that will guide FAA through 2025.

---

[34]The need for stakeholder buy-in and investment, combined with the interdependencies of NextGen improvements, led FAA in 2009 to request that RTCA recommend deliverables to help establish priorities and build support for long-term NextGen investments. RTCA's 2009 NextGen Midterm Implementation Task Force recommendations focused on key improvements that can be implemented with existing technologies and capabilities in the "midterm," which is 2013 through 2018. In 2012, at the request of FAA, the Integrated Capabilities Work Group of the NextGen Advisory Committee (NAC)—a committee comprised of aviation stakeholders from the government and industry and the follow-on to RTCA's Air Traffic Management Advisory Committee—reaffirmed the RTCA task force's recommendations and developed a subset of priority operational improvements for major airports and multi-airport airspace ("metroplexes") that have either the greatest need for improvements or offer the greatest potential benefit to the NAS in the midterm.

[35]The seven are four NextGen programs—ADS-B, Data Communications (Data Comm), NAS Voice System (NVS), and System Wide Information Management (SWIM)—and three NextGen-related programs—En Route Automation Modernization (ERAM), Terminal Automation Modernization and Replacement (TAMR), and Terminal Flight Data Manager (TFDM).

Maintaining the ATC Infrastructure through the Transition to NextGen while Consolidating or Closing Aging Facilities

Stakeholders and FAA officials agree that a challenge for FAA is to maintain the ATC infrastructure through the transition to NextGen while also consolidating or closing aging facilities. Because NextGen represents a transition from existing ATC systems and facilities to new systems, it necessitates changes to or consolidation of existing facilities. Thirty-seven of 76 stakeholders mentioned that consolidating or closing older air traffic control facilities and the need to maintain older "legacy" systems was a challenge. Stakeholders noted congressional interest in preserving ATC facilities and the associated jobs in their districts as a cause for making it more difficult for FAA to close facilities. FAA officials acknowledged that reducing the "footprint" of the air traffic control infrastructure has been difficult but added that they are working on their first set of facility consolidation recommendations, as required by law, and will have those recommendations ready by the end of 2014.[36] In August 2013,[37] we found that if aging systems and associated facilities were not retired, FAA would miss potential opportunities to reduce its overall maintenance costs at a time when resources needed to maintain both systems and facilities may become scarcer and recommended that FAA develop a strategy for implementing the FAA's Air Traffic Organization's (ATO) plans. FAA concurred with this recommendation and is working to develop such a strategy by September 2014. An example of a facility FAA plans to close—a very high frequency omnidirectional radio range (VOR) station—is shown in figure 5.[38]

[36]FAA Modernization and Reform Act of 2012, Pub. L. No. 112-95, § 804, 126 Stat. 11, 119 (2012).

[37]GAO-13-693.

[38]We found that, according to FAA data, the number of unscheduled outages for VORs increased 130 percent between fiscal years 2001 and 2011, and that 9 out of 10 VORs were beyond their useful service life. Because parts for this system can no longer be procured, FAA has to reengineer and construct new parts from existing VOR parts, which is a time- and resource-intensive process—exceeding $110 million per year.

GAO-14-770 Air Traffic Control System

Figure 5: Very High Frequency Omnidirectional Radio Range (VOR) Station

Source: FAA | GA0-14-770

Industry Stakeholders Suggested Changes That Could Improve ATC System Performance and Modernization and Identified Issues to Be Considered If ATC Operations Were Separated from FAA

Stakeholders Suggested Changes to Improve Performance of ATC Operations and Modernization of the ATC

Overall, while stakeholders generally thought the current ATC system was operating at least moderately efficiently under FAA's leadership, when asked what potential changes, if any, to FAA could improve the performance of ATC operations and NextGen implementation, 64 of the 76 stakeholders we interviewed suggested changes. The six most often suggested changes are discussed below. (See app. V for a list and examples of the changes to FAA that the stakeholders suggested during our interviews with them.) Some of these changes address the six challenges raised by stakeholders previously mentioned, while the rest address other challenges stakeholders identified.

Change how FAA Is Funded. The change suggested by the most stakeholders (36 of the 64 stakeholders who suggested a change) was to modify how FAA's ATC operations and NextGen programs are funded. As discussed earlier, budget uncertainty was raised by stakeholders as a challenge for FAA's ATC operations, NextGen modernization, or both. While 36 stakeholders said a change to the funding process or source of funding was needed, most focused on the outcome they would like to see, namely a more stable or predictable funding stream. Fewer stakeholders (11) offered specific suggestions on how to achieve this outcome. For example, one stakeholder suggested providing FAA with a top-line budget number and then allowing FAA to determine how to allocate resources based on its priorities. FAA officials suggested changes to the agency's funding mechanism that could improve FAA's ability to operate the ATC system and implement NextGen, including allowing FAA the flexibility to use funds for their highest priority areas, increasing the fees for registering aircraft, and authorizing FAA to use multi-year funds.

Improve Human Capital Activities. Twenty-four of the 64 stakeholders who suggested a change suggested human capital improvements. Stakeholder suggestions included updating the air traffic controller's handbook, improving the training air traffic controllers receive on new technologies, and streamlining the hiring process. For example, stakeholders said changes were needed to streamline FAA's air traffic controller-training programs and to ensure the best applicants are hired, especially as many current controllers begin to retire. In June 2008, we reported on FAA's efforts to hire and train new controllers, in light of the expected departure, mostly due to retirements, of much of the current air traffic controller workforce of over 15,000 controllers between 2008 and

2017. We also found FAA needed to ensure that technician- and controller-training programs were designed to prepare FAA's workforce to use NextGen technologies.[39] Regarding updating the air traffic controller's handbook, a senior FAA official said that stakeholders do not appreciate what changing the handbook involves, such as running safety scenarios and testing new procedures to ensure any changes do not adversely affect safety. More broadly, another senior FAA official said that shifting to NextGen would require a cultural change in how air traffic controllers are trained to respond to traffic.

Improve Internal Collaboration. Twenty-four of the 64 stakeholders who suggested a change suggested FAA needs to improve internal collaboration within the organization. Stakeholders said different offices within FAA do not communicate well with one another and that this situation has resulted in difficulties and delays in the roll out of NextGen technologies and procedures. Stakeholder suggestions included improving how FAA's lines of business work together to implement NextGen. In August 2013, we found that FAA is making progress in ensuring communication on NextGen issues across lines of business, for example, through the NextGen Management Board and biweekly program review meetings. In the same report, we also discussed how designating one leader, such as the Deputy Administrator's responsibility over NextGen, can improve interagency collaboration and speed decision-making.[40] While external stakeholders raised internal collaboration as an area in need of improvement, FAA senior management said that there are good working relationships between the lines of business responsible for ATC operations and NextGen implementation, especially between the Assistant Administrator of NextGen, the COO of the ATO, and the Associate Administrator of Aviation Safety.

Streamline Processes. Twenty-three of the 64 stakeholders suggesting a change suggested that FAA needs to streamline some of its processes. Stakeholder suggestions included streamlining the development and implementation of flight navigation procedures, the certification of new

---

[39]GAO, *Federal Aviation Administration: Efforts to Hire, Staff, and Train New Air Traffic Controllers Are Generally on Track, but Challenges Remain.* GAO-08-908T (Washington, D.C.: June 11, 2008); GAO-13-693.

[40]GAO-13-693.

aircraft equipment, and the acquisition of new technology. For example, to streamline its process for certifying new technology, one stakeholder said that FAA should use an approach that recognizes that once a type of equipment, such as an antenna, is found to be safe, every piece of that equipment produced does not have to be personally inspected by FAA. FAA officials said that they are making progress streamlining both the certification of new technology and development of new procedures; however, FAA must ensure that new procedures and technology are evaluated for potential safety and environmental concerns and that community outreach occurs. In April 2013, we found that FAA's processes and requirements, while keeping the U.S. airspace safe, are also complex and lengthy. [41] This includes the processes for developing PBN and other new flight navigation procedures. In the April 2013 report, we also found that FAA had efforts under way to address some of these issues, such as the Navigation Lean (NAV Lean) initiative, which is focused on streamlining the implementation and amendment processes for all flight procedures, but it will be several years before the impact is known. In June 2014, the Department of Transportation Inspector General's office found that aviation stakeholders are unlikely to see the full benefits of the NAV Lean initiative, namely a reduction in the time it takes to implement new procedures, until September 2015 or later. [42] In October 2010 and October 2013, we found inefficiencies in the certification and approvals process and variations in FAA's interpretation of certification standards, and recommended improvements FAA could make to evaluate and track certification and approval processes. [43] In October 2013, we also found that while FAA had developed milestones and deployed a tracking system to monitor each certification-related initiative, FAA had not identified overall performance metrics for these efforts to determine whether they would achieve their intended effects. Ultimately, we concluded that having efficient and consistent certification

---

[41]GAO-13-264.

[42]DOT Inspector General, *FAA Faces Significant Obstacles in Advancing the Implementation and Use of Performance-Based Navigation Procedures.* AV-2014-057. June 17, 2014

[43]GAO, *Aviation Safety: Status of Recommendations to Improve FAA's Certification and Approval Process,* GAO-14-142T (Washington, D.C.: Oct 30, 2013); *Aviation Safety: Certification and Approval Processes Are Generally Viewed as Working Well, but Better Evaluative Information Needed to Improve Efficiency,* GAO-11-14 (Washington, D.C.: Oct. 7, 2010).

processes will allow FAA to better use its resources as its workload increases with the implementation of NextGen.[44]

Improve Coordination with Industry Stakeholders. Stakeholders acknowledged the improvements FAA has made in involving stakeholders in the planning and implementation of NextGen initiatives, especially through the NextGen Advisory Committee. However, 23 of the 64 stakeholders who suggested a change suggested FAA should do more to encourage participation and communication with industry stakeholders. For example, one stakeholder said that while FAA has improved its collaboration with industry stakeholders, particularly by including a wider range of stakeholders, FAA needs to ensure that stakeholders are involved early in the planning process for NextGen initiatives. FAA officials said that ensuring the appropriate stakeholders are involved in an effort is a challenge, but noted that FAA has on-going efforts to ensure the right stakeholders are involved to avoid some of the earlier difficulties rolling out NextGen programs. Similarly, in April 2013, we found that FAA is making progress in systematically involving industry stakeholders, air traffic controllers, and other key subject matter experts in its initiatives, such as the OAPM initiative. However, we have also recommended areas for improvement, such as developing and implementing guidelines for ensuring timely inclusion of appropriate stakeholders, including airport representatives, in the planning and implementation of NextGen improvement efforts.[45] DOT concurred with these recommended areas for improvement and is taking steps to implement the recommendations.

Increase Accountability. Twenty-one of the 64 stakeholders who suggested a change suggested FAA needs to increase accountability. Stakeholder suggestions included that FAA should hold its employees and management accountable for how well they accomplish program and plan goals and for how funds are spent. For example, one stakeholder suggested an annual operating plan could help hold FAA accountable to its performance goals. The need for more accountability at FAA, specifically regarding the implementation of NextGen, cuts across several areas we have previously reported on. In February 2014, we found that complex organizational transformations, such as NextGen, require substantial leadership commitment over a sustained period and that

---

[44]GAO-14-142T.

[45]GAO-13-264.

leaders must be empowered to make critical decisions and held accountable for results.[46] In April 2013, we also found that to address accountability issues, FAA has taken steps, such as designating the Deputy Administrator as the Chief NextGen Officer with responsibility for all NextGen activities. In the same report, we also discussed that the use of performance measures would allow stakeholders to hold FAA accountable for results.[47]

While Most Stakeholders Agreed That Separating ATC Operations from FAA Was an Option to Consider, They Identified Several Issues That Would Need to be Taken into Account

In light of the ongoing discussion within the aviation industry on new approaches for operating and modernizing the ATC system, we also asked stakeholders about changing the provision of ATC services to improve ATC efficiency and NextGen implementation. These potential changes include moving the provision of ATC services out of FAA into a separate unit or organization and commercializing ATC services as has been done in Canada. Seventy percent of the stakeholders (53 of 76) agreed that separating ATC operations out from FAA was an option, but half of these stakeholders (26) voiced serious reservations or indicated such a change was unlikely to occur. Stakeholders also cited potential benefits of separating air traffic control operations from FAA, including a more predictable funding source; potentially reduced political involvement in ATC operational decisions; faster and less costly modernization of the ATC system; and more efficient day-to-day operations. The remaining stakeholders we interviewed were split between the opinion that a separate ATC system was not a good idea (12) and either not providing an opinion on this question or not answering it (11). See table 2 below for stakeholder responses. Stakeholders also raised several issues that would need to be taken into account before making changes to the provision of ATC services.

Further, no stakeholder category was unanimous in either supporting or rejecting the option to change provision of ATC services. Airlines were generally more supportive of separating the ATC system from FAA than labor unions and professional associations. General aviation stakeholders were open to the idea but had reservations about the funding scheme. See table 2 for stakeholder responses to this question by industry category. In addition, FAA officials said that they were not opposed to

[46]GAO-14-285T.

[47]GAO-13-264.

privatization or commercialization of the ATC system, but they would rather focus on what services FAA should provide and what is the best way to pay for these services.

Table 2: Stakeholder Responses to GAO Question on Separating Air Traffic Control (ATC) Services from Federal Aviation Administration (FAA) by Industry Category

Do you think that separating the functions of the safety regulator and ATC service provider into separate units or organizations is an option for the United States?

Industry category[a]	Number of stakeholders in category	Yes	Maybe[b]	No	No opinion	No answer given
Airlines	17	9	5	1	2	0
Airports	7	1	3	2	1	0
Aviation experts and other relevant organizations	18	10	6	2	0	0
General aviation	4	1	1	1	0	1
Labor unions and professional associations	8	1	3	2	2	0
Manufacturers and service providers	16	4	5	3	4	0
Other stakeholders	6	1	3	1	0	1
Total	76	27	26	12	9	2

Source: GAO Analysis. | GAO-14-770

[a] We included industry categories with at least 4 interviewed stakeholders or stakeholder organizations. As a result, 3 industry categories—Research and Development Organizations, Other Federal Agencies, and Passenger and Safety Groups—are combined into the Other category.

[b] This answer was not given as a choice. However, because a large number of stakeholders qualified their "Yes" responses with significant reservations, we added it as a category in this table.

Few stakeholders suggested a specific alternative structure for the provision of ATC services, although some listed potential characteristics of an alternative structure, such as user fees, public-private partnership, and a board of directors composed of system users. One example of a specific alternative structure suggested by a stakeholder was a Consumer Service Corporation with no shareholders, so as to avoid vested interests. Others suggested models similar to NAV CANADA, a non-profit trust with a board of representatives made up of industry and government, financed with user fees, and regulated by government.

Both stakeholders and FAA officials said it was important to identify what problem or problems separating ATC services out of FAA is intended to solve, before proceeding with it as a solution. However, if a change were to be made, 65 of the 76 stakeholders suggested actions to take or raised issues or concerns to consider. These issues and concerns include the following:

- *Funding:* Forty of these 65 stakeholders said the source of funding for a separate air traffic control system is important to consider. Stakeholders suggested different sources of revenue to support a separated ATC system including user fees and a fuel tax. Several stakeholders suggested the possibility of accessing funds through capital markets as an advantage of a separated ATC system. Because the expectation of a future revenue stream (through user fees, for example) may enable a corporatized or privatized ATC system to access private capital markets (to obtain, for example, a bond issuance), a potential benefit of such a structure could be more reliable financing for multiyear investment projects as well as for operations.
- *Lessons Learned:* Thirty-eight of these 65 stakeholders suggested studying what the separation of air traffic services from FAA would look like. Stakeholders suggested looking at how air-navigation service providers function in other countries and trying to learn from their successes and mistakes. For example, one stakeholder said that given the efficiency of the current system, before any changes are made, there needs to be an analysis of how privatization would affect passengers, airlines, the aviation industry, and what improvements, including fewer delays and more capacity, it could offer. In a 2005 review of selected foreign air navigation service providers (ANSP), we also found some lessons learned during commercialization, including being prepared to mitigate the financial effects of an industry downturn; the importance of involving industry stakeholders in efforts to design, acquire, and deploy new technologies; balancing the business needs of an ANSP with smaller communities' need for air service; and the importance of maintaining appropriate level of staff to carry out safety regulation.[48]
- *Congressional involvement:* Twenty-nine of these 65 stakeholders suggested that the extent of Congress's role in overseeing a separate ATC system must be clarified. For example, stakeholders said Congress's oversight responsibilities of a separate ATC system and even whether Congress should have oversight of such a system needs to be considered.
- *Regulatory coordination:* Twenty-seven of these 65 stakeholders suggested that ensuring coordination between the safety regulator and a separate ATC system should be considered. Stakeholders

---

[48]GAO-05-769.

noted, for example, that ensuring coordination might be more difficult with a separated ATC system than under the current structure.

- *Governance:* Twenty-five of these 65 stakeholders suggested that governance of a separated ATC system, such as including system users on an oversight body, needs to be considered. For example, one stakeholder asked who would be on a board of directors and how those individuals would be chosen.

- *Safety:* Twenty-four of these 65 stakeholders raised concerns about safety under a separate ATC system. Stakeholders were concerned about several issues, including the effect of a non-governmental operator's profit motive on safety and whether requiring users to pay a fee to use air traffic control services may disincentivize use of the system.

- *Transition management:* Twenty-one of these 65 stakeholders raised concerns about how to transition from the current system to a separate ATC system. Stakeholder concerns included the length and difficulty of such a transition and included questions about what to do with the infrastructure and personnel in the current system, and the modernization efforts already under way. FAA senior management also cited transition management as a potential impediment to moving to a different air traffic control structure. Specifically, an FAA official said there does not appear to be an understanding by those advocating privatization of how to move from a government-operated system to a privatized system given the need to operate the NAS at a high level of safety and efficiency. FAA officials also raised concerns about the length and difficulty of such a transition. For example, one official mentioned that such a transition to a new organization would have to include cultural and personnel changes and could take many years to implement. Another official was concerned that a transition occurring now to a privatized system could negatively affect the implementation of NextGen. In November 2002, we found that successful change management initiatives in large private and public sector organizations can often take at least 5 to 7 years.[49]

- *Access:* Nineteen of these 65 stakeholders also raised concerns about access to the NAS under a separate ATC system. For example, stakeholders were concerned about small communities losing access to the ATC system and that the fees charged by a separate ATC system might reduce general aviation's access to the ATC system.

---

[49]GAO, *Highlights of a GAO Forum: Mergers and Transportation: Lessons Learned for a Department of Homeland Security and Other Federal Agencies*, GAO-03-293SP (Washington, D.C.: Nov. 14, 2002).

Agency Comments

We provided DOT with a draft of this report for its review and comment. DOT provided technical comments, which we incorporated as appropriate.

We are sending copies of this report to the appropriate congressional committees, the Secretary of the Department of Transportation, and other interested parties. In addition, the report is available at no charge on the GAO website at http://www.gao.gov.

If you or your staff members have any questions about this report, please contact me on (202) 512-2834 or at dillinghamg@gao.gov. Contact points for our Offices of Congressional Relations and Public Affairs may be found on the last page of this report. Key contributors to this report are listed in appendix VI.

Gerald L. Dillingham, Ph.D.
Director, Physical Infrastructure Issues

Appendix I: Objectives, Scope, and Methodology

Our work for this report focused on aviation stakeholders' perspectives on the performance of the air traffic control (ATC) system and efforts to modernize it. This report examines stakeholder perspectives on: (1) the performance of the current ATC system and its modernization through the NextGen initiative, and any challenges the Federal Aviation Administration (FAA) may face in managing these activities; and (2) potential changes, if any, that could improve the performance of the ATC system, including FAA's modernization initiative. We were also asked to obtain stakeholders' perspectives on the safety of the National Airspace System (NAS). However, since nearly all stakeholders we interviewed agreed that the NAS is extremely or very safe, we did not focus on this area in this report.

To obtain aviation stakeholders' perspectives on these issues, we interviewed a non-probability sample of 76 aviation stakeholders. We created an initial list of stakeholders using internal knowledge of the aviation industry. We then added more stakeholders based on interviewee responses to our question on whom else they thought we should speak with. Specifically, we wanted to obtain perspectives from individuals and organizations with direct experience, as users, or knowledge, through research or study, of the current ATC system, modernization efforts, and FAA's management of the system. As such, we limited our review to U.S.-based companies and airlines and sought the views of individuals and organizations with a stake in the performance of the NAS. We divided stakeholders into the following nine categories: airlines, airports, aviation experts and other relevant organizations, general aviation, labor unions and professional associations, manufacturers and service providers, other federal government agencies (Department of Defense and National Aeronautics and Space Administration (NASA)), passenger and safety groups, and research and development organizations. A list of the individuals and groups we interviewed is in appendix II. We used a semi-structured interview format with both closed- and open-ended questions to obtain aviation stakeholder perspectives on the efficiency of the current ATC, implementation of NextGen, and changes, if any, that could improve the operation of the ATC and implementation of NextGen. Our interview format contained four closed-ended questions with either a five-level scale or a yes/no response. These closed-ended questions, the response categories, and stakeholder responses are either included in the body of the report or in appendix III, as appropriate.

The intent of our open-ended questions was to engage the stakeholders in a conversation about the issues they considered most important and

relevant. The results of our review are not generalizable to the industry as
a whole.

Our discussion of the challenges FAA faces, potential changes to FAA,
and issues to consider if the ATC system were separated from FAA is
based on stakeholder responses to our open-ended questions. As such,
the numbers we reported with these items represent those stakeholders
that raised a challenge or issue to consider or suggested a change during
our interview. When we report that 43 stakeholders raised budget
uncertainty as a challenge, this does not necessarily mean that the
remaining 33 stakeholders we interviewed disagreed. Rather, it means
that those stakeholders did not raise it during the course of our interview.

We analyzed the responses to these open-ended questions to identify the
main themes raised by stakeholders. To ensure the accuracy of our
content analysis, we internally reviewed our coding and reconciled any
discrepancies. In discussing stakeholder responses to our open-ended
questions, we aggregated their responses and reported on stakeholders'
perspectives in general.

Stakeholder responses to the yes-no question: Do you think that
separating the functions of safety regulator and ATC service provider into
separate units or organizations is an option for the United States?—fell
into four general responses, which we describe in this report as yes;
maybe; no; and no opinion. Respondents who answered "yes" to this
question said that separating the ATC service provider from the safety
regulator (FAA) was not only an option, but also a good idea. While these
respondents still provided issues to consider, they said that this option
should be considered and were generally supportive of it. GAO classified
respondents' answers as "Maybe" for those who answered that this was
an option, but generally said either it was not a good idea, it was not
feasible in the United States, or that they had very strong reservations
about such a change.

Respondents who answered "no" generally said that it was a bad idea or
would simply not work in the United States. Finally, some respondents
indicated that they had "no opinion," meaning that their organization did
not have an official position on whether this change was an option in the
United States.

We reported on stakeholder responses to this closed-ended question—
Do you think that separating the functions of the safety regulator and ATC
service provider into separate units or organizations is an option for the

United States?—by industry category. For the three industry categories
with fewer than four respondents—other federal government agencies,
passenger and safety groups, and research and development
organizations—we combined these into one category and refer to them in
table 2 as Other stakeholders.

To obtain FAA senior management views on the preliminary results of our
content analysis of stakeholder perspectives, we conducted semi-
structured interviews with: Administrator; Deputy Administrator/Chief
NextGen Officer; Assistant Administrator for NextGen; Associate
Administrator for Aviation Safety; Chief Operating Officer (COO) of the Air
Traffic Organization (ATO); and Assistant Administrator for Policy,
International Affairs, and Environment.

We reviewed GAO reports and other sources of aviation information to
provide context to the challenges raised by the stakeholders and their
suggested changes to the current structure. We identified reports that had
discussed the stakeholder-identified themes, including collaboration with
stakeholders, delivery of NextGen capabilities, and Performance-Based
Navigation procedures, and FAA leadership in overseeing NextGen
implementation.

We conducted this performance audit from November 2013 to September
2014 in accordance with generally accepted government auditing
standards. Those standards require that we plan and perform the audit to
obtain sufficient, appropriate evidence to provide a reasonable basis for
our findings and conclusions based on our audit objectives. We believe
that the evidence obtained provides a reasonable basis for our findings
and conclusions based on our audit objectives.

Appendix II: List of the 76 Aviation Industry Stakeholders GAO Interviewed

Category	Subcategory	Stakeholder
Airlines	Associations	Airlines for America (A4A)
		Cargo Airline Association (CAA)
		National Air Carrier Association (NACA)
		Regional Airline Association (RAA)
		Regional Air Cargo Carriers Association (RACCA)
	Cargo	FedEx
		United Parcel Service (UPS)
	Passenger	Alaska Airlines
		American Airlines
		Delta Air Lines
		JetBlue Airways
		Southwest Airlines
		United Airlines
	Regional passenger	American Eagle Airlines
		Air Wisconsin Airlines Corporation
		Cape Air
		Endeavor Air
Airports	Airport operators	Dallas/Fort Worth International Airport
		Houston Airport System (George Bush Intercontinental Airport, William P. Hobby Airport, and Ellington Airport)
		Los Angeles World Airports (Los Angeles International Airport, LA/Ontario International Airport, and Van Nuys Airport)
		Metropolitan Airports Commission (Minneapolis-St. Paul International Airport)
		Port Authority of New York and New Jersey (John F. Kennedy International Airport, Newark Liberty International Airport, LaGuardia Airport, Stewart International Airport, and Teterboro Airport)
	Associations	Airports Council International—North America (ACI-NA)
		American Association of Airport Executives (AAAE)
Aviation experts and other relevant organizations		Bill Ayer, Chair of the NextGen Advisory Committee (NAC)
		Air Traffic Control Association (ATCA)
		Michael Baiada, President and Chief Executive Officer, ATH Group
		Gary Church, President, Aviation Management Associates
		Dr. George Donohue, Systems Engineering and Operations Research, George Mason University
		Michael Dyment, Managing Partner, NEXA Capital Partners, LLC
		Amr ElSawy, President and Chief Executive Officer, Noblis Inc.
		Dr. John Fearnsides, Chief Executive Officer, MJF Strategies, LLC

Category	Subcategory	Stakeholder
		Dr. Mark Hansen, Civil and Environmental Engineering, University of California, Berkley
		Dr. John Hansman, Aeronautics and Astronautics, Massachusetts Institute of Technology
		Metron Aviation
		Robert Poole, Director of Transportation Policy, Reason Foundation
		RTCA (formerly known as the Radio Technical Commission for Aeronautics)
		Dr. Stephen Van Beek, Vice President, ICF International
	Former FAA officials	J. Randolph Babbitt, Former Administrator (2009-2011)
		Russell Chew, Former Chief Operations Officer, Air Traffic Organization (2003-2007)
		Richard Day, Former Senior Vice President of Operations, Air Traffic Organization (2008-2010)
		David Grizzle, Former Chief Operations Officer, Air Traffic Organization (2011-2013)
General aviation		Aircraft Owners and Pilots Association (AOPA)
		Helicopter Association International (HAI)
		National Air Transportation Association (NATA)
		National Business Aviation Association (NBAA)
Labor unions and professional associations		Air Line Pilots Association (ALPA)
		Allied Pilots Association (APA)
		Coalition of Airline Pilots Associations (CAPA)
		FAA Managers Association
		National Air Traffic Controllers Association (NATCA)
		NetJets Association of Shared Aircraft Pilots (NJASAP)
		Professional Aviation Safety Specialists (PASS)
		Southwest Airlines Pilots' Association (SWAPA)
Manufacturers and service providers	Aircraft	Beechcraft
		Boeing
		Cessna Aircraft Company
		Gulfstream Aerospace Corporation
	Associations	Aerospace Industries Association (AIA)
		Aircraft Electronics Association (AEA)
		General Aviation Manufacturers Association (GAMA)
	Aviation equipment and systems	General Electric (GE) Aviation
		Harris Corporation
		Honeywell Aerospace

Category	Subcategory	Stakeholder
		Exelis
		Mosaic ATM
		Raytheon
		Rockwell Collins
		Thales
		United Technologies (UTC) Aerospace Systems
Other federal government agencies		Department of Defense (DOD)
		National Aeronautics and Space Administration (NASA)
Passenger and safety groups		Flight Safety Foundation
		Travelers United (formerly Consumer Travel Alliance)
Research and development organizations		MITRE Center for Advanced Aviation System Development (CAASD)
		Volpe: The National Transportation Systems Center—Air Traffic Systems and Operations

Source: GAO. | GAO-14-770

Appendix III: Responses to GAO's Closed-Ended Question on Safety

How would you characterize the safety of the current National Airspace System, including the operations of the Air Traffic Control system

Safety rating	Number of stakeholder responses
Extremely	41
Between very to extremely[a]	9
Very	21
Moderately	2
Marginally	0
Not very	0
No rating given	3
Total	**76**

Source: GAO Analysis. | GAO-14-770

[a]This rating was not given to the stakeholders as a choice; however, the stakeholders' answers fell between these categories.

Appendix IV: List of Challenges FAA Faces in
Improving the Efficiency of the Air Traffic Control (ATC)
System and Implementing NextGen, as Raised by the
76 Aviation Industry Stakeholders GAO Interviewed

Challenge for FAA	Description and examples of challenge cited by stakeholders	Number of stakeholders citing challenge
Ensuring aircraft are equipped to take advantage of NextGen	Due to the expense and uncertainty over FAA's ability to meet timelines for deploying NextGen technologies users have been reluctant to equip their aircraft	46
Mitigating the effects of an uncertain fiscal environment	Budget uncertainty makes it difficult for FAA to continue operation of an efficient ATC system and/or implement NextGen	43
Human capital activities	FAA does not match workforce skills with needs for hiring and staffing, provides insufficient training, and has insufficient planning for upcoming retirements	42
Implementing new navigation procedures	FAA's development and implementation of PBN-related procedures is not working well or is moving too slowly.	41
Articulating what NextGen is and delivering benefits in the near term	FAA must continue to deliver systems, procedures, and capabilities that demonstrate near-term benefits and returns on users' investments to convince aviation system users to make investments in NextGen equipment.	40
Maintaining the ATC infrastructure through the transition to NextGen while consolidating or closing aging facilities	FAA must plan for changes to or consolidation of existing facilities because NextGen represents a transition from existing ATC systems and facilities to new systems.	37
Intra-agency coordination or communication	FAA's offices are stove-piped, do not share information with each other well, or are not horizontally integrated.	32
Risk-averse culture	FAA's aversion to risk and focus on safety prevents improvements in efficiency and adoption of new technologies and procedures.	29
Handling irregular operations	FAA does not handle ATC operations well when airspace capacity is affected by congestion and disruptions due to, for example, inclement weather and power outages.	29
Congress	Congress politicizes FAA's budget and micromanages FAA operations.	28
Organizational structure	FAA's organizational structure misplaces offices and blurs lines of authority and responsibilities.	24
Coordination and communication with external stakeholders	FAA does not communicate, coordinate, or collaborate well with the aviation industry.	21
Planning	FAA does not plan well, such as setting unrealistic deadlines, or its plans lack clarity and precision.	21
Leadership	FAA's leadership and political appointees lack the right professional background and experience.	21
Surface operations and infrastructure	FAA does not operate airport surface operations well to accommodate increased air capacity or maintain surface infrastructure well.	21
General policies and procedures	FAA's policies and procedures are not up-to-date or lack clarity.	16
Consistency across the ATC system	FAA controllers in different regions and airports are not consistent in applying procedures, such as approach and departure procedures.	15
Accountability	There is little accountability in FAA, such as for NextGen delays.	12

Appendix IV: List of Challenges FAA Faces in
Improving the Efficiency of the Air Traffic
Control (ATC) System and Implementing
NextGen, as Raised by the 76 Aviation Industry
Stakeholders GAO Interviewed

Challenge for FAA	Description and examples of challenge cited by stakeholders	Number of stakeholders citing challenge
Certification processes	FAAs' process for certifying safety, aircraft, avionics, and personnel takes too long, or is inconsistent.	12
Performance measures	FAA lacks adequate performance measures or its measures are output-related, instead of outcome-related.	11

Source: GAO. | GAO-14-770

Note: We included challenges that were raised by more than 10 stakeholders.

Appendix V: List of Changes to FAA to Improve the Efficiency of the Air Traffic Control (ATC) System or the Implementation of NextGen, or Both, as Cited by the 76 Aviation Industry Stakeholders GAO Interviewed

Change to FAA	Examples of suggested changes	Number of stakeholders suggesting change
Change how FAA is funded	FAA needs a more stable or predictable funding stream.	36
Improve human capital activities	FAA needs to improve human capital activities including updating the air traffic controller handbook, improving the training air traffic controllers receive on new technologies, and streamlining the hiring process.	24
Improve internal collaboration	FAA needs to improve communication within the agency to reduce difficulties and delays in the roll out of NextGen technologies and procedures.	24
Streamline processes	FAA needs to streamline the development and implementation of flight navigation procedures, the certification of new aircraft equipment, and the acquisition of new technology.	23
Improve coordination with industry stakeholders	While FAA has made improvements involving stakeholders in the planning and implementation of NextGen initiatives, FAA should do more to encourage participation and communication with industry stakeholders.	23
Increase accountability	FAA should hold its employees and management accountable for how well they accomplish program and plan goals and for how funds are spent.	21
Improve leadership at FAA	There needs to be consistent and empowered leadership at FAA.	16
Change role and responsibility of NextGen Office	FAA needs to ensure that all NextGen activities are overseen by one NextGen office.	13
Create performance measures	FAA needs to create relevant performance measures that measure improvements resulting from the implementation of NextGen.	11
Deliver capabilities with near-term benefits	FAA needs to focus on delivering NextGen capabilities with near-term benefits.	8
Change FAA's oversight of industry	FAA needs to reconsider how it oversees the industry and/or reduce its layers of oversight.	6

Source: GAO. | GAO-14-770

Appendix VI: GAO Contact and Staff Acknowledgments

GAO Contact	Gerald L. Dillingham, Ph.D., (202) 512-2834, or dillinghamg@gao.gov
Staff Acknowledgments	In addition to the individual named above, Catherine Colwell, Assistant Director; Amy Abramowitz; Sarah Arnett; William Colwell; Kevin Egan; Sam Hinojosa; David Hooper; Stuart Kaufman; Jennifer Kim; Josh Ormond; Amy Rosewarne; and Rebecca Rygg made key contributions to this report.

Related GAO Products

NextGen

FAA Reauthorization Act: Progress and Challenges Implementing Various Provisions of the 2012 Act. GAO-14-285T. Washington, D.C.: February 5, 2014.

National Airspace System: Improved Budgeting Could Help FAA Better Determine Future Operations and Maintenance Priorities. GAO-13-693. Washington, D.C.: August 22, 2013.

NEXTGEN Air Transportation System: FAA Has Made Some Progress in Midterm Implementation, but Ongoing Challenges Limit Expected Benefits. GAO-13-264. Washington, D.C.: April 8, 2013.

Next Generation Air Transportation System: FAA Faces Implementation Challenges. GAO-12-1011T. Washington, D.C.: September 12, 2012.

Air Traffic Control Modernization: Management Challenges Associated with Program Costs and Schedules Could Hinder NextGen Implementation. GAO-12-223. Washington, D.C.: February 16, 2012.

Next Generation Air Transportation: Collaborative Efforts with European Union Generally Mirror Effective Practices, but Near-term Challenges Could Delay Implementation. GAO-12-48. Washington, D.C.: November 3, 2011.

Next Generation Air Transportation System: FAA Has Made Some Progress in Implementation, but Delays Threaten to Impact Costs and Benefits. GAO-12-141T. Washington, D.C.: October 5, 2011.

NEXTGEN Air Transportation System: Mechanisms for Collaboration and Technology Transfer Could Be Enhanced to More Fully Leverage Partner Agency and Industry Resources. GAO-11-604. Washington, D.C.: June 30, 2011.

Aviation Safety and Certification

Aviation Safety: Status of Recommendations to Improve FAA's Certification and Approval Processes. GAO-14-142T. Washington, D.C.: October 30, 2013.

Facilities

FAA Facilities: Improved Condition Assessment Methods Could Better Inform Maintenance Decisions and Capital-Planning Efforts. GAO-13-757. Washington, D.C.: September 10, 2013.

International Air Navigation Service Providers

Air Traffic Control: Characteristics and Performance of Selected International Air Navigation Service Providers and Lessons Learned from Their Commercialization. GAO-05-769. Washington, D.C.: July 29, 2005.

GAO's Mission	The Government Accountability Office, the audit, evaluation, and investigative arm of Congress, exists to support Congress in meeting its constitutional responsibilities and to help improve the performance and accountability of the federal government for the American people. GAO examines the use of public funds; evaluates federal programs and policies; and provides analyses, recommendations, and other assistance to help Congress make informed oversight, policy, and funding decisions. GAO's commitment to good government is reflected in its core values of accountability, integrity, and reliability.
Obtaining Copies of GAO Reports and Testimony	The fastest and easiest way to obtain copies of GAO documents at no cost is through GAO's website (http://www.gao.gov). Each weekday afternoon, GAO posts on its website newly released reports, testimony, and correspondence. To have GAO e-mail you a list of newly posted products, go to http://www.gao.gov and select "E-mail Updates."
Order by Phone	The price of each GAO publication reflects GAO's actual cost of production and distribution and depends on the number of pages in the publication and whether the publication is printed in color or black and white. Pricing and ordering information is posted on GAO's website, http://www.gao.gov/ordering.htm. Place orders by calling (202) 512-6000, toll free (866) 801-7077, or TDD (202) 512-2537. Orders may be paid for using American Express, Discover Card, MasterCard, Visa, check, or money order. Call for additional information.
Connect with GAO	Connect with GAO on Facebook, Flickr, Twitter, and YouTube. Subscribe to our RSS Feeds or E-mail Updates. Listen to our Podcasts. Visit GAO on the web at www.gao.gov.
To Report Fraud, Waste, and Abuse in Federal Programs	Contact: Website: http://www.gao.gov/fraudnet/fraudnet.htm E-mail: fraudnet@gao.gov Automated answering system: (800) 424-5454 or (202) 512-7470
Congressional Relations	Katherine Siggerud, Managing Director, siggerudk@gao.gov, (202) 512-4400, U.S. Government Accountability Office, 441 G Street NW, Room 7125, Washington, DC 20548
Public Affairs	Chuck Young, Managing Director, youngc1@gao.gov, (202) 512-4800 U.S. Government Accountability Office, 441 G Street NW, Room 7149 Washington, DC 20548

Please Print on Recycled Paper.